IN THE RAINFOREST

Written and illustrated by **KATE DUKE**

HARPER

An Imprint of HarperCollins Publishers

For Sidney, always
—K.D.

The Let's-Read-and-Find-Out Science book series was originated by Dr. Franklyn M. Branley, Astronomer Emeritus and former Chairman of the American Museum–Hayden Planetarium, and was formerly co-edited by him and Dr. Roma Gans, Professor Emeritus of Childhood Education, Teachers College, Columbia University. Text and illustrations for each of the books in the series are checked for accuracy by an expert in the relevant field. For more information about Let's-Read-and-Find-Out Science books, write to HarperCollins Children's Books, 195 Broadway, New York, NY 10007, or visit our website at www.letsreadandfindout.com.

Let's Read-and-Find-Out Science® is a trademark of HarperCollins Publishers.

In the Rainforest

Copyright © 2014 by Kate Duke

Manufactured in China.

ISBN 978-0-06-028259-2 (trade bdg.) — ISBN 978-0-06-445197-0 (pbk.)

The artist used pen and ink, watercolor, liquid acrylic, pencils, and pastels on Arches watercolor paper to create the illustrations for this book.

14 15 16 17 18   SCP   10 9 8 7 6 5 4 3 2 1
❖
First Edition

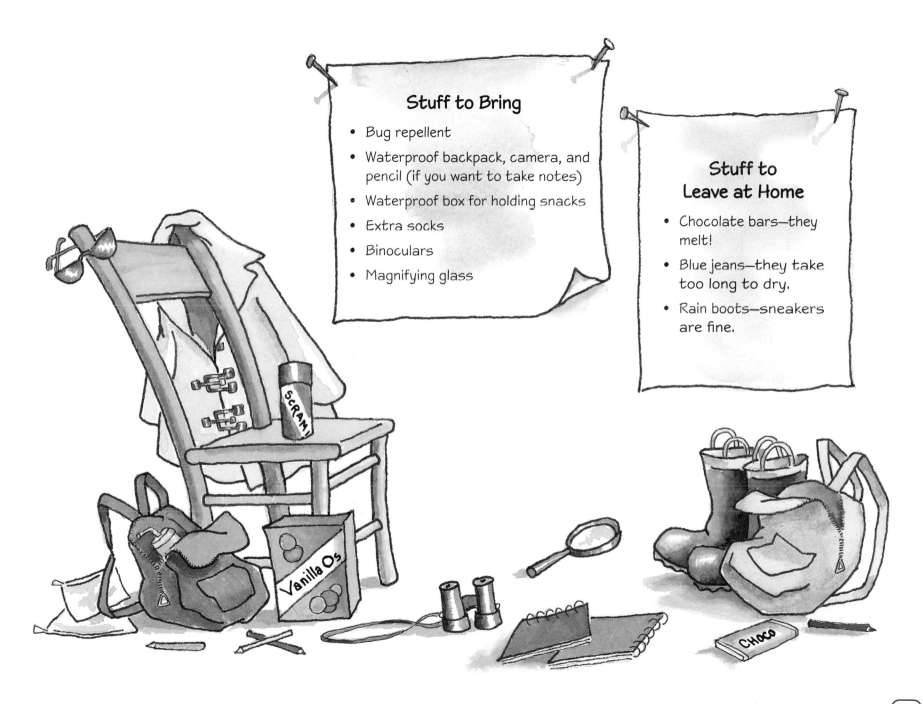

Stuff to Bring

- Bug repellent
- Waterproof backpack, camera, and pencil (if you want to take notes)
- Waterproof box for holding snacks
- Extra socks
- Binoculars
- Magnifying glass

Stuff to Leave at Home

- Chocolate bars—they melt!
- Blue jeans—they take too long to dry.
- Rain boots—sneakers are fine.

In a **tropical** rainforest, there is no spring, summer, fall, or winter. It's warm all the time. There's more rain—and also more sunshine—in tropical rainforests than anywhere else.

Plants can grow all year round, unlike those in forests with **temperate** climates, where there are different seasons.

More plants and more different types of plants grow in tropical rainforests than anyplace else on earth.

How much more rain?

Temperate climates get 20–30 inches of rain a year. A tropical rainforest gets TEN TIMES that much—about 200 inches a year.

That's a lot of water.

No, THIS is a lot of water!

The forest floor is covered with a layer of dead leaves and twigs, called **leaf litter**. Because there's no winter, most trees and plants don't lose their leaves all at once. Instead, they drop a few leaves all year round. Leaf litter is important. In the warm, damp rainforest it quickly rots and turns to compost, which is plant food. This compost is vital to the forest. **Vital** means "life-giving." The trees and plants need compost to grow.

> The forest floor may be covered with dead leaves, but it is full of life.

Rainforests need MORE food than temperate forests.

The layer of leaf litter and compost-rich soil is only a few inches deep. With so many plants, the forest uses up the food *very* quickly.

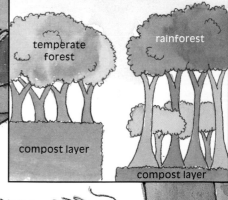

temperate forest

rainforest

compost layer

compost layer

Some leaf-litter critters

Hercules beetle

Up to 7 inches long

Dung beetle

Collects animal droppings

Centipede • Can grow to 12 inches

The forest floor is very shady. The plants down here are called **understory** plants, because they are able to grow *under* taller plants that block the light. Even without much sun, their leaves can get very big.

Hey, my sneakers are still dry. I thought a rainforest would be like a swamp.

Nope. The thick layer of leaves up above keeps a lot of the rain from getting down here, except during the rainiest months.

Besides plants, millions of animal species live in rainforests. Surprisingly few are mammals. Some of the larger mammals live only on the forest floor and in the understory. But you probably won't see them. They're hiding from another understory mammal—the jaguar, the largest rainforest cat.

Keep looking!

I don't even see one mammal!

But you may not see a jaguar, either. They're hiding, too—waiting to jump out and catch the other mammals.

The part of the forest above the understory is called the **canopy**. There's more sun up there, and it's much more crowded with plants and animals.

It's not easy to get up into the canopy, because it's so high. Scientists use ropes and clamps to climb the huge trees.

These vines are called *lianas*. They crisscross the forest, growing from tree to tree.

You're doing great!

I've climbed trees at home, but nothing like this!

Eek!

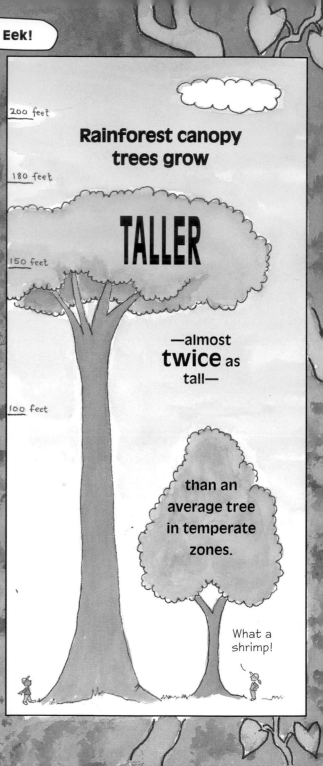

200 feet

180 feet

150 feet

100 feet

Rainforest canopy trees grow

TALLER

—almost **twice** as tall—

than an average tree in temperate zones.

What a shrimp!

Look! A tadpole! And a lizard! And a snake! Dragonflies! Beetles! Ants!

Keep going! I've counted over 200 species living in epiphytes like this one!

Under this platform, there's a special kind of plant called an **epiphyte**.

Epiphytes grow on other plants, instead of on the ground.

They have hardly any roots at all. They get their food and water from the air.

Howler monkeys come to drink from the "tank."

And a crab! A crab living in a tree!

Many epiphytes are shaped to catch rainwater in the spaces between their leaves.

A big one can hold up to ten gallons of water. These epiphytes are sometimes called **tank plants**, because they are like storage tanks for water to be shared by the creatures living in the canopy.

Birds drink and hunt here.

An epiphyte can start growing in a little crack in tree bark.

Mosses growing on trees are epiphytes.

There are MORE kinds of epiphytes in rainforest canopies around the world than anywhere else.
How many?
At least
30,000!

Across the canopy, water-storing epiphytes grow everywhere. They cover the tree trunks, they sit on branches, and they balance on twigs. They even grow on other epiphytes. Millions of canopy animals depend on the tank plants' water supply. The animals drink it, lay eggs in it, swim in it, and catch food in it. Some of them make nests or hiding places among the epiphytes' leaves. Without these plants, all these frogs, lizards, snakes, insects, mammals, and birds would have a tough time staying alive. The canopy would be a much emptier place.

A bat! Finally— a mammal!

Epiphyte growing on an epiphyte

Wow! A baby jaguar!

No, it's a MARGAY, the smallest cat in this rainforest. Jaguars don't climb this high.

Some ferns are epiphytes.

Orchids can be epiphytes.

Scientists and explorers have found MORE animal species in rainforest canopies than anywhere else on earth:

- HUNDREDS of birds, reptiles, and amphibians
- DOZENS of kinds of mammals
- 1 MILLION insect species, and probably millions more still undiscovered

Some canopy animals stay in the trees their whole lives. Their feet may never touch the ground even once. They travel easily on "liana highways" to find food and water—everything they need—a hundred feet or more in the air.

Coatis sometimes travel upside down.

Climb even higher and you'll be above the canopy. This is called the **emergent layer**, because it's where the tallest trees *emerge*, or stick out, above the rest. Your head will be emerging from the branches into the sunshine.

This is the part of the rainforest that gets the most sun. You'll be hotter than you ever thought you could be!

Blue morpho butterfly

Emergent tree

Bee

Hummingbird

Wasp

Just a few of the thousands of pollinators in the rainforest

The leaves of the upper canopy trees are small and tough, to stand up to the heat of the sun.

It can be really windy at the top of the rainforest, but most rainforest plants are not pollinated by wind. Instead, they depend on animals—usually flying animals like birds and insects—for pollination. Fruit-eating birds and bats also help spread seeds through their droppings.

Black-throated trogon

Scarlet macaw

Butterfly

Bat

Beetle

Moth

More pollinators

The more you look around the canopy, the more different kinds of insects you will see. Scientists have found that there are more insects in tropical rainforests than any other kind of animal.

Maybe you don't like insects. Get over it! They are *very* important. Take ants, for instance. Ants live in every part of the rainforest.

Eggs

Nest area

Ants attacking a beetle

These **Azteca ants** make nests inside tree branches. They protect their homes by attacking the tree's enemies, like beetles and caterpillars, that could eat up all its leaves.

Other ants live on the forest floor, like these **army ants**. Usually they don't make nests. Instead, the whole colony—more than half a million ants—camps out and hunts together in a huge group, capturing everything in sight: frogs, lizards, beetles, grasshoppers, ants, mice, and wasps.

Army ants help keep the forest floor from getting too crowded.

Army ants can't kill humans, but they do bite. Better not to get too close.

Army ants help birds catch a meal. These birds are called antbirds (surprise!).

Eyelash viper

Forest scorpion

Skink

Poison dart frog

19

Do you see these little brown ants? They live underground, under the forest floor, but all day, every day, they leave their tunnels and travel up the tall tree trunks and down again. Each one brings back a little piece of green that it has cut from a leaf. They are called **leaf-cutter ants**.

Wow! It's three feet tall . . .

Here is the nest under this anthill. Well—it's not exactly an anthill, is it? It's an ant *mountain*.

The leaf-cutters built this ant mountain. How could such tiny creatures make something so big? The leaf-cutter ants are tiny, but there are a lot of them!

As many as 5 million of them may live in a single colony. And they work nonstop.

. . . and more than eight feet across!

They've carried out about 80,000 pounds of soil to create this mountain.

Leaf-cutters dig tunnels that can go down as much as twenty feet. The mountain is made from all the dirt that they dug out to make the tunnels.

The tunnels lead to rooms where the leaf-cutter ants store the cut leaves.

One nest can have more than a thousand rooms.

The ants in a big colony like this will bring in about a hundred pounds of leaves each day. They use the leaves to make their food.

Another kind of
anteater

Not all leaf-cutter mounds are so big. But the ants' work is important. Their mounds make patches of soft, loose soil where plants can grow. The "garbage" they carry out—tons of used-up leaves and fungus—adds compost.

There can be thousands of leaf-cutter colonies in a rainforest, with billions of workers plowing up the soil. Because of their digging, rainwater is able to soak into the ground more easily. The ants help the trees and other plants stay alive.

The soil a few inches under the leaf litter is thick clay, with no nutrients to feed plant roots.

Rodents, earthworms, and some beetles dig shallow tunnels.

25

Now you've seen a tropical rainforest from top to bottom, and underneath, too. It's divided into four parts: the forest floor, the understory, the canopy, and the emergent layer. But the parts are definitely NOT divided from each other. Instead, they depend on one another. And they all depend on the rain.

canopy becomes home for millions of species,

rain fills tank plants,

trees grow tall, canopy grows thick,

Warm rain falls, speeds up leaf litter decay,

decayed litter becomes compost, feeds plant roots,

canopy plants flower,
make seeds,

leaves fall,
seeds drop,

composted leaf litter helps seeds sprout,
new trees and plants grow.

The rain makes the canopy grow thick and green. Leaves fall from the canopy and fertilize the forest floor. The litter feeds the roots of the trees. The trees then grow more leaves—leaves for leaf eaters, plus flowers for pollinators, fruit for fruit eaters, and perches for epiphytes, all of which keep the canopy thick and green. Everything gets recycled. Everything balances out. The rainforests of the world are incredibly old. Left alone, it's likely that they could go on forever.

But the rainforests may not go on forever, because people are cutting them down all over the world as fast as they can. Sometimes people clear rainforest land to try to make farms. Sometimes companies cut the trees to sell the wood. They don't understand that cutting the forest makes the perfectly balanced system fall apart.

It looks like a desert.

Where are all the animals?

Take away the trees, and all the animals and plants that live in them and on them, around them and under them, will have nowhere to live anymore, and they'll die. Take away the trees and plants, and all the roots that held the soil together disappear. Without them, the thin layer of good soil quickly gets washed away by all the rain.

The bare dirt underneath gets hard. The sun bakes it harder, until nothing can grow in it except a few grasses and weeds. Once it is gone, a natural rainforest can never come back.

Toucan

Luckily there are still a lot of rainforests left in many parts of the world. And a lot of people are trying to keep them healthy. Some are scientists who want to study and learn from the life in the forests. Some are people who think rainforests are beautiful and amazing, something that should not be lost forever. They will have to work hard, but they believe that rainforests are worth it.

What do you think?

Some Useful Rainforest Discoveries So Far

- Chocolate
- Vanilla
- Bananas
- Pineapples
- Cinnamon
- Sugar
- Rice
- Pepper
- Oranges
- Coffee
- Dyes
- Plant fibers to make cloth
- Plant fibers for building materials
- Fibers for making bulletproof vests
- Rubber
- Medicines
- Tea

Rainforest Discoveries of the Future

- Who knows?

FIND OUT MORE ABOUT THE RAINFOREST

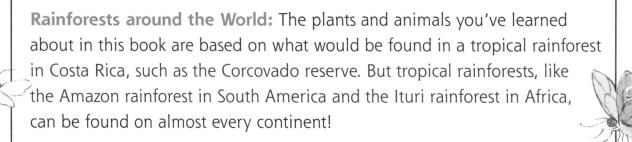

Rainforests around the World: The plants and animals you've learned about in this book are based on what would be found in a tropical rainforest in Costa Rica, such as the Corcovado reserve. But tropical rainforests, like the Amazon rainforest in South America and the Ituri rainforest in Africa, can be found on almost every continent!

Visit a Rainforest!

Many botanical gardens, museums, and zoos around the United States have rainforest exhibits where you can see some of the plants, insects, and animals mentioned in this book. Here are a few:

- **Rainforests of the World at the California Academy of Science,** *San Francisco, CA* (www.calacademy.org/academy/exhibits/rainforest)

- **The Butterfly Rainforest at the Florida Museum of Natural History,** *Gainesville, FL* (www.flmnh.ufl.edu/exhibits/always-on-display/butterfly-rainforest)
- **Amazonia at the Smithsonian National Zoo,** *Washington, DC* (http://nationalzoo.si.edu/Animals/Amazonia)
- **The Tropical Pavilion at the Brooklyn Botanic Garden,** *Brooklyn, NY* (www.bbg.org/discover/gardens/tropical_pavilion)

- You can also see leaf-cutter ant colonies at these locations!
  Audubon Butterfly Garden and Insectarium, *New Orleans, LA* (www.auduboninstitute.org/visit/insectarium) Click on the Ant Cam!
  Peabody Museum Discovery Room, *New Haven, CT* (http://peabody.yale.edu/education/discovery-room)

Make your own rainforest terrarium!

What's a terrarium? A terrarium is a mini-ecosystem, made out of a sealed container with plants inside. Similar to a real rainforest, the terrarium you will build is a humid, warm plant environment that is self-contained and self-sustaining. You'll be able to observe the terrarium watering itself as it processes water into vapor (evaporation) and from vapor into water (precipitation) in a water cycle.

Materials:

- A clear container that can be sealed (a plastic container with a lid, a fish tank with a cover, even a soda bottle works!)
- Small rocks or pebbles
- Enough activated charcoal to make a ½-inch layer inside the container. This is found in pet stores.
- Sphagnum moss
- Potting soil, found at garden centers and some hardware stores. Make sure it does not have added fertilizer.
- Miniature varieties of ferns like button ferns, Scottish or Irish moss, miniature African violets, and even Venus flytraps! You can find these in a plant nursery or garden center.
- Water

Procedure:

1. Fill the bottom of the container with a 1-inch-deep layer of small rocks or pebbles.
2. Layer the activated charcoal on top of the pebbles or stones. Be sure not to mix the two layers. The charcoal should form a layer about ½ inch deep.
3. Take your sphagnum moss and layer it on top. You can add sticks and bark to the moss so it's even more like a real rainforest floor. You don't need to add a lot of moss, but make sure it's thick enough to prevent any water from leaking through to the pebbles below.
4. Carefully spoon your soil in so you won't disturb the bottom layers of your terrarium. The soil needs to support the plants' roots, so make sure it's at least 2 inches deep.
5. Plant your mosses, ferns, and other small plants in the soil. You can also add in some decorations—rocks, bark, or even your favorite plastic animals.
6. Slowly trickle a small amount of water down the side of your container until the soil is moist. It's very important not to overwater, so take your time when adding water.
7. Wait until all the leaves on all your plants are dry and then seal the lid.
8. Place the rainforest in a spot that receives indirect sunlight most of the day, like a windowsill.
9. Be sure to open the lid and let some fresh air circulate every couple of weeks to prevent mold from growing. Water once a month and watch your ecosystem grow!

This book meets the Common Core State Standards for Science and Technical Subjects.

Be sure to look for all of these books in the Let's-Read-and-Find-Out Science series:

STAGE 1

The Human Body:
How Many Teeth?
I'm Growing!
My Feet
My Five Senses
My Hands
Sleep Is for Everyone

Plants and Animals:
Animals in Winter
Baby Whales Drink Milk
Big Tracks, Little Tracks
Bugs Are Insects
Dinosaurs Big and Small
Ducks Don't Get Wet
Fireflies in the Night
From Caterpillar to Butterfly
From Seed to Pumpkin
From Tadpole to Frog
How Animal Babies Stay Safe
How a Seed Grows
A Nest Full of Eggs
Starfish
A Tree Is a Plant
What Lives in a Shell?
What's Alive?
What's It Like to Be a Fish?
Where Are the Night Animals?
Where Do Chicks Come From?

The World Around Us:
Air Is All Around You
The Big Dipper
Clouds
Is There Life in Outer Space?
Pop!
Snow Is Falling
Sounds All Around
What Makes a Shadow?

STAGE 2

The Human Body:
A Drop of Blood
Germs Make Me Sick!
Hear Your Heart
The Skeleton Inside You
What Happens to a Hamburger?
Why I Sneeze, Shiver, Hiccup, and Yawn
Your Skin and Mine

Plants and Animals:
Almost Gone
Ant Cities
Be a Friend to Trees
Chirping Crickets
Corn Is Maize
Dolphin Talk
Honey in a Hive
How Do Apples Grow?
How Do Birds Find Their Way?
Life in a Coral Reef
Look Out for Turtles!
Milk from Cow to Carton
An Octopus Is Amazing
Penguin Chick
Snakes Are Hunters
Spinning Spiders
Sponges Are Skeletons
What Color Is Camouflage?
Who Eats What?
Who Lives in an Alligator Hole?
Why Do Leaves Change Color?
Why Frogs Are Wet
Wiggling Worms at Work
Zipping, Zapping, Zooming Bats

Dinosaurs:
Did Dinosaurs Have Feathers?
Digging Up Dinosaurs
Dinosaur Bones
Dinosaur Tracks
Dinosaurs Are Different
Fossils Tell of Long Ago
My Visit to the Dinosaurs
What Happened to the Dinosaurs?
Where Did Dinosaurs Come From?

Space:
Floating in Space
The International Space Station
Mission to Mars
The Moon Seems to Change
The Planets in Our Solar System
The Sky Is Full of Stars
The Sun
What Makes Day and Night
What the Moon Is Like

Weather and the Seasons:
Down Comes the Rain
Feel the Wind
Flash, Crash, Rumble, and Roll
Sunshine Makes the Seasons
Tornado Alert
What Will the Weather Be?

Our Earth:
Archaeologists Dig for Clues
Earthquakes
Follow the Water from Brook to Ocean
How Mountains Are Made
In the Rainforest
Let's Go Rock Collecting
Oil Spill!
Volcanoes
What Happens to Our Trash?
What's So Bad About Gasoline?
Where Do Polar Bears Live?
Why Are the Ice Caps Melting?
You're Aboard Spaceship Earth

The World Around Us:
Day Light, Night Light
Energy Makes Things Happen
Forces Make Things Move
Gravity Is a Mystery
How People Learned to Fly
Light Is All Around Us
Switch On, Switch Off
What Is the World Made Of?
What Makes a Magnet?
Where Does the Garbage Go?

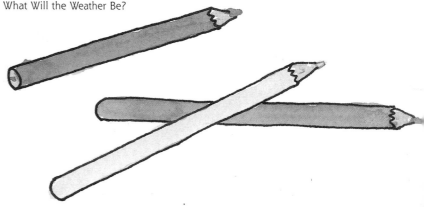